FIRST MAN
ON THE MOON

Ben Hubbard

WAYLAND
waylandbooks.co.uk

First published in Great Britain in 2019
by Wayland
Copyright © Hodder & Stoughton 2019

Credits
Editor: Julia Bird
Illustrator: Alex Orton
Packaged by: Collaborate

ISBN 978 1 5263 1066 8

Wayland
An imprint of Hachette Children's Group
Part of Hodder & Stoughton
Carmelite House
50 Victoria Embankment
London EC4Y 0DZ
www.hachette.co.uk

Printed in China

FSC
www.fsc.org

MIX
Paper from
responsible sources
FSC® C104740

CONTENTS

MAN INTO SPACE

In 1961 the world received amazing news. The Soviet Union had just launched the first man into space. On 12 April, cosmonaut Yuri Gagarin blasted off from Earth aboard a small, round spacecraft called Vostok 1. The Vostok mission to orbit the Earth was the most dangerous and ambitious space challenge yet attempted.

As Vostok 1 sped around the Earth at 28,800 km per hour, Gagarin's pencil began floating in front of him. "Weightlessness has begun. It's not at all unpleasant," Gagarin reported. But trouble was ahead. After an hour, Vostok 1 began spinning out of control as it prepared to re-enter Earth's atmosphere. The spacecraft became red-hot and Gagarin struggled not to pass out. As Vostok 1 hurtled towards Earth, Gagarin blew its explosive hatch and parachuted safely to the ground.

The success of Vostok 1 made a hero of Yuri Gagarin. At the time, the USA was locked in a competition with the Soviet Union to conquer space, known as the Space Race. Now, the USA had to show that it too could send a man into space.

A few weeks after Gagarin landed, the USA launched a man into space for 15 minutes. But then American president John F. Kennedy made an extraordinary announcement: "This nation should commit itself to achieving the goal, before the decade is out, of landing a man on the Moon and returning him safely to Earth." Kennedy's speech stunned America's rocket scientists. They had only just sent a man into space. Now they had less than nine years to get a man to the Moon and back.

RACE FOR ROCKETS

President Kennedy's surprise pledge to put men on the Moon seemed an impossible task. Only four years earlier, the USA did not even have the technology to send a rocket into space. Instead, the Soviet Union had beaten them to this goal when it launched satellite Sputnik 1 aboard an R-7 rocket.

The Soviet R-7 rocket was based on the V-2 missile used by the Nazis during the Second World War (1939–1945). The V-2 was a long-range terror weapon that could carry one ton of explosives for over 320 kilometres. Then, at four times the speed of sound, the V-2 would drop silently on cities such as London.

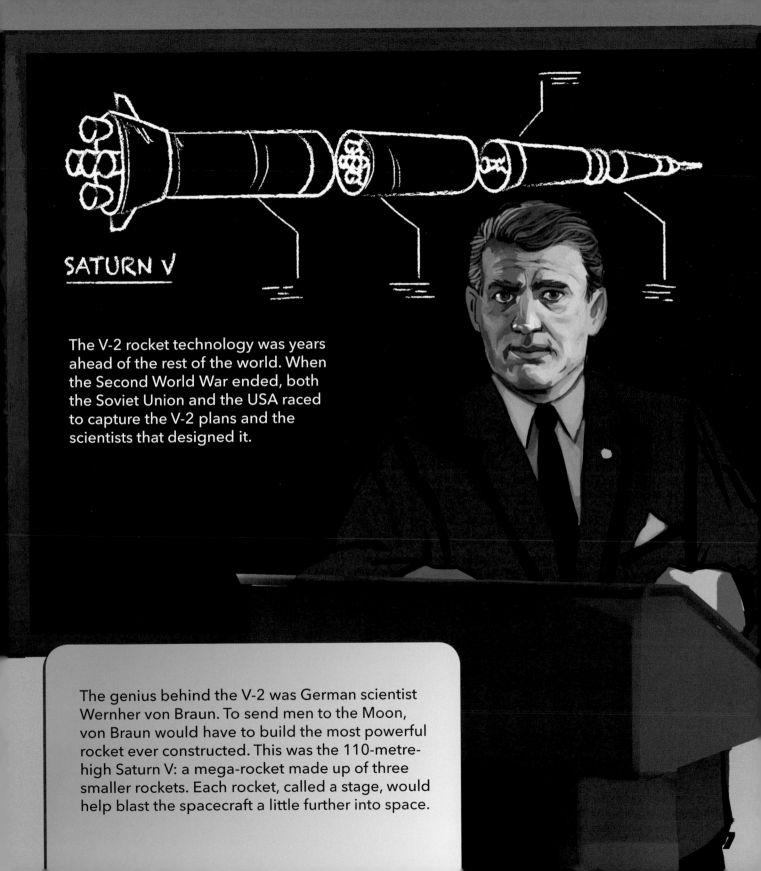

SATURN V

The V-2 rocket technology was years ahead of the rest of the world. When the Second World War ended, both the Soviet Union and the USA raced to capture the V-2 plans and the scientists that designed it.

The genius behind the V-2 was German scientist Wernher von Braun. To send men to the Moon, von Braun would have to build the most powerful rocket ever constructed. This was the 110-metre-high Saturn V: a mega-rocket made up of three smaller rockets. Each rocket, called a stage, would help blast the spacecraft a little further into space.

ASTRONAUT ARMSTRONG

No-one knew what America's astronauts might encounter in space, so only top fighter pilots like Neil Armstrong, Buzz Aldrin and Michael Collins were invited to try out for training. But first, they faced some tough and sometimes strange tests.

For one test, Armstrong was told to stand in a bucket of ice as ice water was squirted into his ear. Next, he had to calculate a period of two hours while shut in an isolation chamber with no light, sound or smell. Finally, Armstrong was locked in a room where the temperature reached a scorching 63 degrees Celsius.

Armstrong, Aldrin and Collins all passed their tests and were invited to train as astronauts for the Apollo Moon programme. Here, their training included rides on the dreaded centrifuge machine. This span astronauts around at tremendous speeds so they could experience the G-force, or 'Gs', felt at lift-off. Most people passed out at 9Gs, but Armstrong could withstand an eye-watering 15Gs.

In space there is no gravity and so the astronauts would become weightless. In the early 1960s, no-one could be sure what this felt like. To find out, the astronauts practised aboard a reduced-gravity aircraft. The aircraft flew to a high altitude and then dropped suddenly in a roller-coaster type free-fall. This created a few seconds of weightlessness on board – and often caused astronauts to lose their lunch. The aircraft soon became known as the 'Vomit Comet' as a result!

THE FLYING BEDSTEAD

To reach the Moon, the Apollo astronauts would have to land a Lunar Module on its surface. The practice vehicle looked like a bed frame and it was quickly nicknamed the 'Flying Bedstead'. It was a dangerous machine to fly, however.

To train on the Bedstead, the Apollo astronauts had to fly it over 150 metres above the ground. A crash at this height could be fatal. There had already been several accidents before Neil Armstrong began his training flight on it. Armstrong flew to the correct height, but as he brought the Bedstead down to land, it began spinning dangerously out of control.

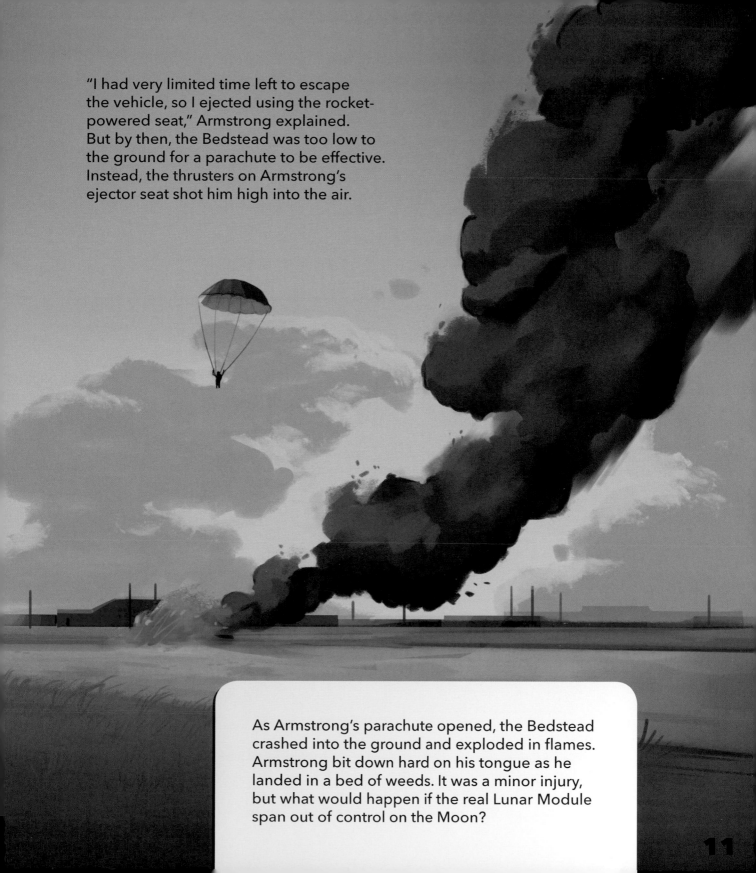

"I had very limited time left to escape the vehicle, so I ejected using the rocket-powered seat," Armstrong explained. But by then, the Bedstead was too low to the ground for a parachute to be effective. Instead, the thrusters on Armstrong's ejector seat shot him high into the air.

As Armstrong's parachute opened, the Bedstead crashed into the ground and exploded in flames. Armstrong bit down hard on his tongue as he landed in a bed of weeds. It was a minor injury, but what would happen if the real Lunar Module span out of control on the Moon?

DOCKING DISASTER

Returning from the Moon was as risky as getting there. The Apollo astronauts would have to blast off in the Lunar Module and connect with a spacecraft waiting in the Moon's orbit. To practise, a rocket was launched into space. Then, 100 minutes later, Gemini VIII was sent after it, flown by Neil Armstrong. His mission: to catch the rocket and dock with it in space.

It took several hours for the spacecraft to catch up with the rocket, as both sped around the Earth. At last Gemini VIII and the rocket connected and both spacecraft began flying in space as one. Then, suddenly, radio contact with Armstrong was lost. Gemini VIII and the rocket had gone into a roll.

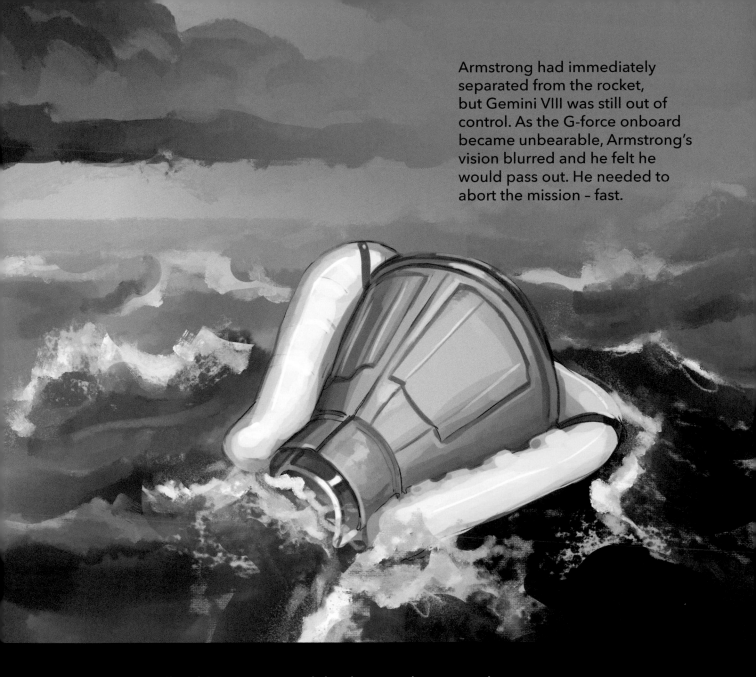

Armstrong had immediately separated from the rocket, but Gemini VIII was still out of control. As the G-force onboard became unbearable, Armstrong's vision blurred and he felt he would pass out. He needed to abort the mission – fast.

Armstrong radioed Mission Control that he was about to make an emergency landing. He jammed on the re-entry thrusters and Gemini VIII slowed down quickly. But as the spacecraft fell towards Earth, Armstrong had little control where it would land. As the spacecraft's parachutes opened, Armstrong was relieved to glimpse blue below him: the Pacific Ocean. Gemini VIII splashed down safely, but Armstrong became violently seasick as the spacecraft was tossed around in the rough seas. The

COUNTDOWN

By mid-1969, the Apollo mission training was over. On the morning of 16 July, Neil Armstrong, Buzz Aldrin and Michael Collins prepared to board the Apollo 11 spacecraft that would take them to the Moon. Over 400,000 people had worked tirelessly for eight years to make President Kennedy's Moon deadline a reality. Now, the moment of truth had arrived. At 28 hours before lift-off, or "T minus 28 hours", the countdown began …

T-8 HOURS 32 MINUTES

Rocket fuel is loaded into Apollo 11's Saturn V rocket.

T-28 HOURS

System checks start and the official countdown begins.

T-3 HOURS 57 MINUTES

The astronauts climb into their spacesuits. They will not breathe fresh air for another eight days.

T-4 HOURS 32 MINUTES

The three astronauts have a breakfast of steak, scrambled eggs, toast, coffee and orange juice.

T-2 HOURS 40 MINUTES

The astronauts climb aboard Apollo 11 and wait for lift-off.

T-15 MINUTES

Final checks are completed and Apollo 11 switches to internal power.

T-9 SECONDS

A white cloud of smoke billows from underneath the Saturn V rocket as its engine ignition sequence begins.

WE HAVE LIFT-OFF!

T-0 SECONDS

A roar fills the air as Apollo 11 lifts from its launch pad. A voice from Mission Control shouts out over the radio: *"We have lift-off! We have lift-off!"*

IN SPACE

As Apollo 11 lifted slowly from its launch pad, the G-force pushed the astronauts back into their seats. Around them was a deafening roar as the rocket rumbled and shook. But slowly, the noise and shaking eased as the rocket blasted towards space. It would take three days to reach the Moon. But to land on the Moon and then return to Earth, Apollo 11 had to perform a series of complex manoeuvres. Each one had to be perfectly timed as there was not enough fuel or oxygen onboard for mistakes.

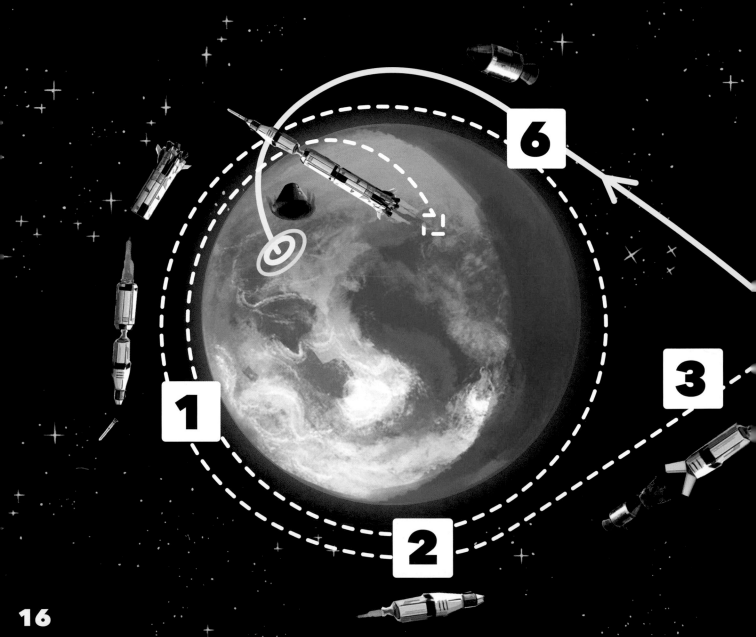

1 Following lift-off, Apollo 11 discards its first two stages and orbits the Earth 1.5 times.

2 Apollo's third stage fires it out of Earth's orbit and towards the Moon.

3 Apollo's Command and Service Module (CSM) detaches, turns around and pulls out the Lunar Module from inside the third stage. The third stage is discarded.

4 Apollo begins orbiting the Moon. Astronauts Armstrong and Aldrin detach in the Lunar Module, called *Eagle*, and land it on the Moon. Collins stays aboard the CSM in the Moon's orbit.

5 The Lunar Module splits in two. Its ascent stage takes off from the Moon and docks with the CSM. The CSM then fires its rockets back towards Earth.

6 As the CSM re-enters Earth's atmosphere, the Command Module (CM) separates from the Service Module (SM) and splashes down into the Pacific Ocean.

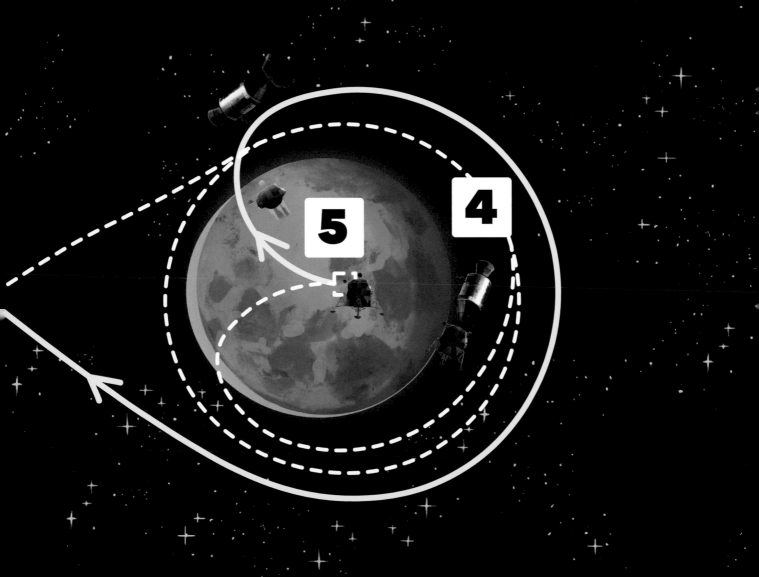

THE MOON LANDING

On 20 July 1969 Neil Armstrong and Buzz Aldrin prepared to land on the Moon's surface. But something was wrong aboard the Lunar Module. Warning alarms flashed from *Eagle's* control panel. Armstrong looked through the window. The *Eagle* had missed its landing spot and was heading towards some rocks. Worse still, the module was running out of fuel.

"You have 60 seconds left of fuel," Mission Control called over the radio, as Armstrong frantically looked for a place to land. Armstrong was NASA's most experienced pilot, but his spacesuit sensors showed his heart rate had jumped to a rapid 156 beats per minute. "Thirty seconds of fuel," called out Mission Control. Then the radio fell silent. Everyone held their breath.

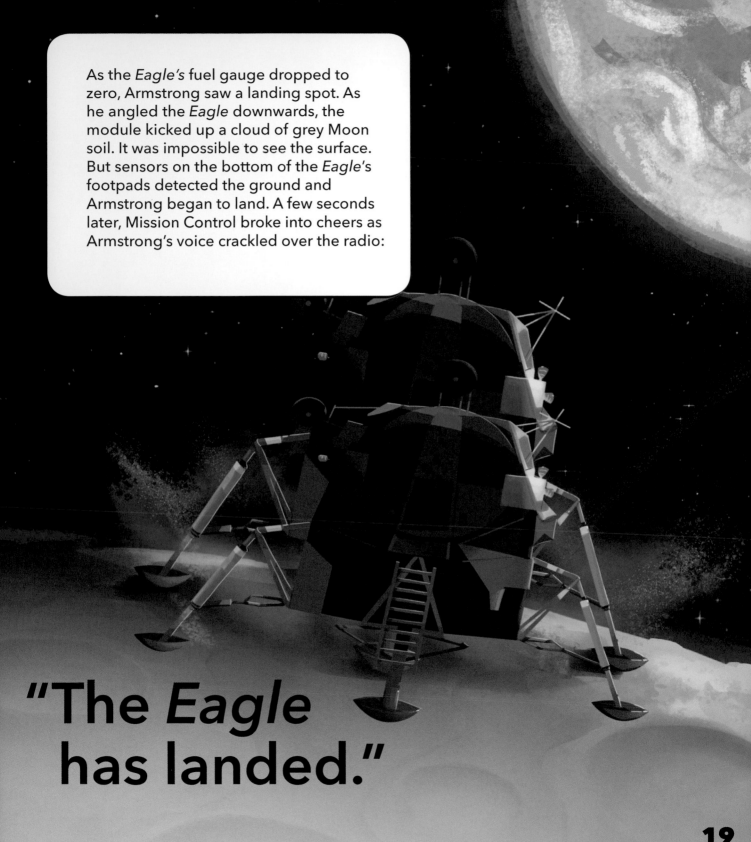

As the *Eagle's* fuel gauge dropped to zero, Armstrong saw a landing spot. As he angled the *Eagle* downwards, the module kicked up a cloud of grey Moon soil. It was impossible to see the surface. But sensors on the bottom of the *Eagle's* footpads detected the ground and Armstrong began to land. A few seconds later, Mission Control broke into cheers as Armstrong's voice crackled over the radio:

"The *Eagle* has landed."

ON[E] [S]MALL ST[EP]

Over 600 million people on Earth had nervously watched the Moon landing live on television. Now they all looked on in amazement as Neil Armstrong lowered himself down the *Eagle's* ladder. As Armstrong became the first human to step onto another planet, he uttered some famous words:

"That's one small step for (a) man, one giant leap for mankind."

As Aldrin climbed down to join Armstrong, he joked about not accidentally locking the Module hatch behind him. At the bottom, the two astronauts paused to gaze at the desert-like lunar landscape. Without an atmosphere to provide wind or rain, Armstrong's first footprint could remain on the Moon for millions of years.

The lack of atmosphere on the Moon made it a hostile place for the astronauts. To protect them, the astronauts' spacesuits were designed like mini spacecraft, with systems to provide oxygen and regulate temperature. On the Moon, temperatures range from 121 degrees to -156 degrees Celsius. There was some good news, however. Both astronauts noticed how light their bulky spacesuits had become. With only one sixth of the gravity on Earth, the Moon made a 163-kg spacesuit feel like only 27 kg.

WORKING ON THE MOON

After taking photos and experimenting with long, low-gravity leaps, Aldrin and Armstrong were sharply reminded they only had 2.5 hours to do their jobs. Both set about collecting soil samples and setting up experiments that would beam back information about the Moon to Earth. They then hammered an American flag into the hard lunar ground. It sent a strong message about the USA's greatest space accomplishment.

With the flag planted, Mission Control warned the astronauts their time on the Moon's surface was up. Armstrong reluctantly began climbing the Lunar Module ladder. "I'd like to stay a little longer, because there are other things I'd like to look at," Armstrong thought.

Aldrin and Armstrong began preparing to leave. They threw everything they didn't need outside the Lunar Module to save weight and left plaques behind to commemorate their trip to the Moon. A medal was left too, as a reminder of Yuri Gagarin, who had died in a flying accident in 1968.

One thing the astronauts could not discard was the Moon dust they had brought back into the Module. Some at Mission Control worried that this dust could ignite and blow up the spacecraft. Then, as they prepared to leave, Armstrong broke an engine switch. This was fixed with a pen, but people were becoming nervous about the astronauts returning safely to Earth. After seven hours of sleep, their countdown to lift-off began.

EARTH BOUND

On board the Command and Service Module, Michael Collins was nervous. It was his job to dock with the Lunar Module. But docking didn't always go to plan. Worse still, the CSM had no landing gear. If the *Eagle* couldn't take off, Collins would not be able to save Armstrong and Aldrin. "… One little hiccup and they are dead men," Collins thought.

On Earth, there was also nervousness at Mission Control. The Module's one lift-off thruster had never before been fired. Now it had to do its job perfectly or the mission to get men to the Moon and back would fail.

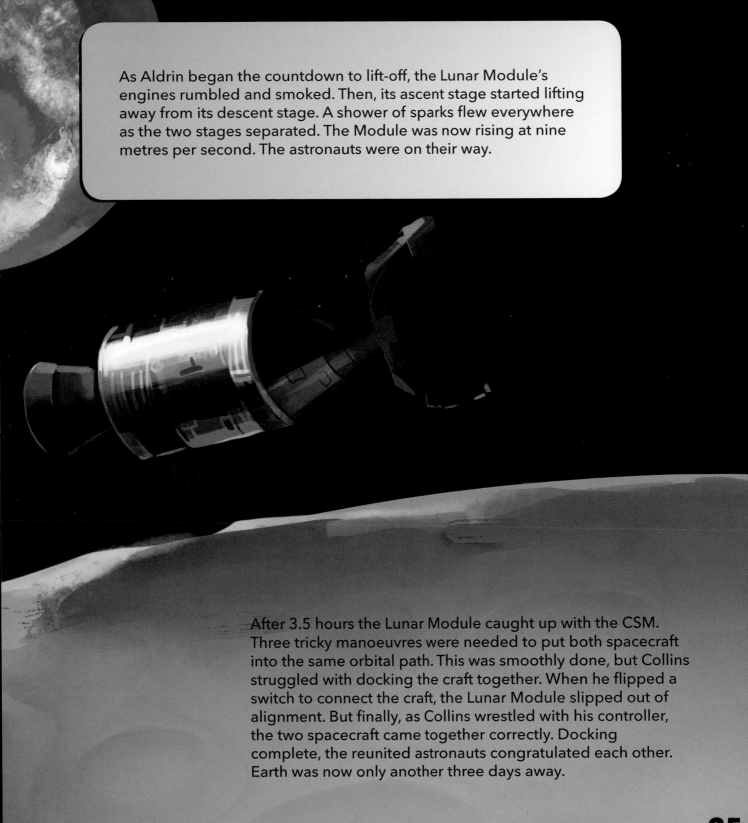

As Aldrin began the countdown to lift-off, the Lunar Module's engines rumbled and smoked. Then, its ascent stage started lifting away from its descent stage. A shower of sparks flew everywhere as the two stages separated. The Module was now rising at nine metres per second. The astronauts were on their way.

After 3.5 hours the Lunar Module caught up with the CSM. Three tricky manoeuvres were needed to put both spacecraft into the same orbital path. This was smoothly done, but Collins struggled with docking the craft together. When he flipped a switch to connect the craft, the Lunar Module slipped out of alignment. But finally, as Collins wrestled with his controller, the two spacecraft came together correctly. Docking complete, the reunited astronauts congratulated each other. Earth was now only another three days away.

SPLASH DOWN

On 24 July, Apollo 11 prepared to land back on Earth. But a dangerous storm threatened the spacecraft's splashdown in the Pacific Ocean. As it descended through the Earth's atmosphere, Apollo 11 was ordered to change its landing site coordinates. It did so as it travelled at a speed of 40,000 km per hour. The CSM then discarded its Service Module and turned itself around so its heat shield was facing forward.

Despite the speed, the astronauts onboard felt like they were moving in slow motion. The blackness of space was replaced with a tunnel of colours – violet, orange, greens and then white clouds and the blue sea below.

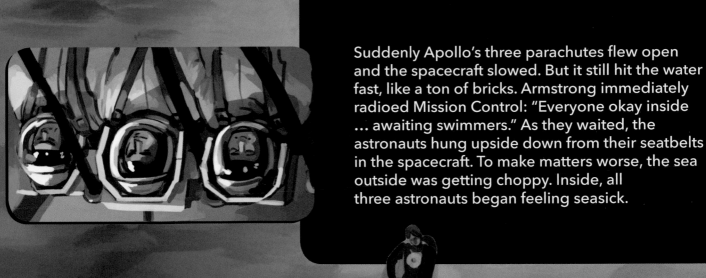

Suddenly Apollo's three parachutes flew open and the spacecraft slowed. But it still hit the water fast, like a ton of bricks. Armstrong immediately radioed Mission Control: "Everyone okay inside ... awaiting swimmers." As they waited, the astronauts hung upside down from their seatbelts in the spacecraft. To make matters worse, the sea outside was getting choppy. Inside, all three astronauts began feeling seasick.

After 29 long minutes, divers reached Apollo 11. They attached a sea anchor and flotation collar to the craft to stabilise it. Now the hatch was opened and the astronauts were given protective suits to wear before they climbed out. Feeling seasick and light-headed as they readjusted to Earth's gravity, the astronauts emerged from the craft one by one. They were lifted on to a helicopter and taken to the nearby US aircraft carrier *Hornet*. Mission complete!

SPACE HEROES

Once on board, the astronauts were locked inside a Mobile Quarantine Facility (MQF) for 16 days as doctors checked that they were not contaminated with any lunar germs. They were visited by their families and even the US President Richard Nixon.

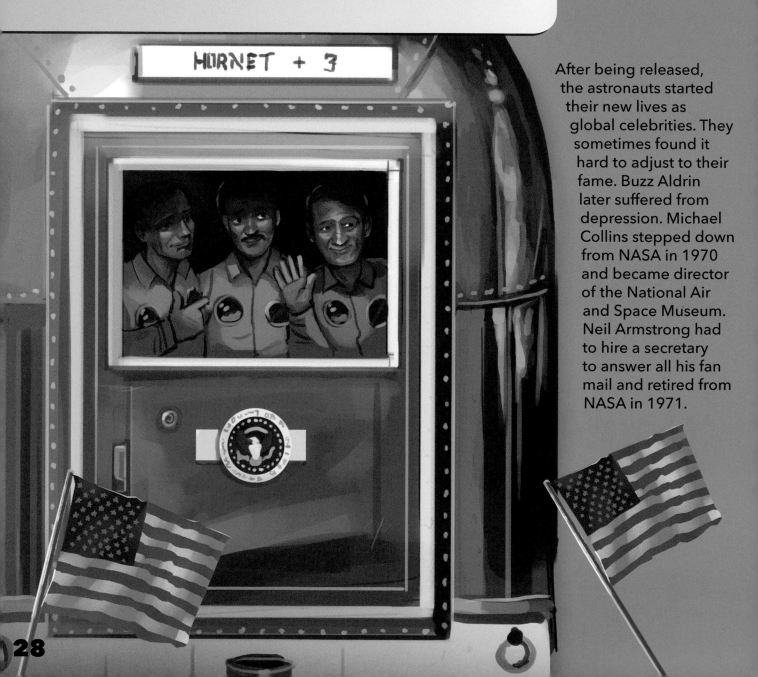

HORNET + 3

After being released, the astronauts started their new lives as global celebrities. They sometimes found it hard to adjust to their fame. Buzz Aldrin later suffered from depression. Michael Collins stepped down from NASA in 1970 and became director of the National Air and Space Museum. Neil Armstrong had to hire a secretary to answer all his fan mail and retired from NASA in 1971.

A further five Apollo missions sent ten more US astronauts to the Moon, before the programme was cancelled in 1972. At that time the USA was fighting an increasingly unpopular war in Vietnam. Many Americans felt that the Apollo programme, which cost over US$12.3 billion, was a waste of money.

Despite winning the Space Race, tensions remained high between the USA and the Soviet Union during the early 1970s. Then, in an attempt to relax the rivalry, the nations agreed to a space docking of an Apollo and Soviet Soyuz spacecraft in July 1975. This gesture put an official end to the Space Race and paved the way for cooperation in space between the two nations. However, no human has set foot on the Moon again since Apollo 17 departed in 1972.

TIMELINE

1944: Nazi Germany fires its first V-2 rockets at targets in England and France.

1955: The Soviet Union builds its top secret Baikonur Cosmodrome to launch space rockets from.

1957: The Soviet Union launches the first satellite into space, Sputnik 1.

1958: The United States launches its first satellite into space, Explorer 1.

1959: NASA astronauts begin weightlessness training.

April, 1961: Yuri Gagarin becomes the first man into space aboard Vostok 1.

May, 1961: The United States launches Alan Shepard into sub-orbit for 15 minutes aboard Freedom 7.

May, 1961: President Kennedy announces the US will land a man on the Moon by the end of the decade.

1962: Neil Armstrong becomes one of the NASA astronauts selected for the Gemini missions.

February, 1962: Astronaut John Glenn becomes the first American to orbit the Earth, flying Friendship 7.

1963: Soviet cosmonaut Valentina Tereshkova becomes the first woman into space aboard Vostok 6.

1965: Cosmonaut Alexei Leonov performs the first spacewalk outside his Voskhod 2 spacecraft.

January, 1967: During routine testing of Apollo 1, astronauts Virgil Grissom, Ed White and Roger Chaffee are killed in a fire.

April, 1967: Soviet cosmonaut Vladimir Komarov is killed during re-entry to Earth, when his Soyuz 1 parachute fails.

November, 1967: the first Saturn V rocket is successfully launched into space.

1968: Apollo 8 becomes the first spacecraft to travel around the Moon and back.

1969: Commander of Apollo 11, Neil Armstrong, becomes the first man to set foot on the Moon.

1972: Apollo 17 becomes the last NASA mission to the Moon.

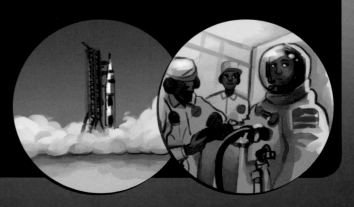

GLOSSARY

Ascent
The act of rising upwards.

Astronaut
A person who is trained to travel into space.

Atmosphere
The protective layer of gases that surrounds the Earth.

Centrifuge machine
A machine that spins rapidly around to inflict a G-force on the person riding it.

Contaminated
Make something impure by exposing it to germs or poisons.

Cosmonaut
An astronaut belonging to the space programme of Russia, previously known as the Soviet Union.

Descent
The act of going downwards.

Discard
Throw away.

Dock
When a spacecraft joins with a space station or another spacecraft in space.

G-force
Short for 'gravity-force'.

Isolation
Being kept away from other people.

Manoeuvre
A series of moves which require great skill.

Memorial
A statue or plaque which reminds people of a particular time, person or event.

Orbit
The curved path an object takes around a planet, moon or star, as a result of gravity.

Rivalry
The competition between two people, groups, or countries to achieve a similar goal.

Soviet Union
The former union of Russia and 14 other states, officially known as the Union of Soviet Socialist Republics (USSR).

Weightlessness
Not feeling the pulling-down effects of gravity.

INDEX